# Content Spinning 101

## A Simple & Valuable Skill in the Digital Age

by Johnna Russell

# Table of Contents

# Preface

I began this book with the intention of teaching people how to spin content. What I've discovered in the land of spinning is that while I may find it fun, like turning writing into a game, it doesn't click as easily for others. For many, simply looking at spintax for the first time is enough to send the mind wandering.

There are plenty of videos and tutorials, but none seem to form an adequate and basic introduction from an angle that teaches the simplicity before the complexity. My goal is to introduce you to the concept and process of content spinning, while allowing you the opportunity to consider the pros, cons, and controversy of doing so in the first place. There is certainly money to be made, whether you spin your own content, hire others to do so for you, or work as a professional content spinner for clients.

The surprising truth about content spinning is that it is among the simplest of tasks, once you learn how to do it. I am no genius, but learned the skill on my own with a quickness reserved for people who need to pay bills and feed children before things go from bad to worse. It worked out alright for me, and it might be just the thing for you.

I hope that by the end of this book, you have a good understanding of the process and are able to decide whether it will be of use for your own purposes.

# Introduction

Content spinning is a means of taking one original item of content, typically an article or blog post, and turning it into spintax, from which dozens, hundreds, or thousands of unique versions can be created.

When your content is in spintax form, and you generate the desired number of unique articles or posts, they will each express the same concepts, the same primary point, the same overall meaning, but in a way that is as unique to each article as you choose to make it.

I'll start by showing you an example of the results of spun content by spinning a small amount of original content and showing you the results only, which may be a less confusing introduction to spinning than the spintax that you will quickly become familiar with.

We'll also take a look at what sort of hat you'll be wearing while you do the job, which is primarily up to you, but something to think about before you really get started. I will then break down the concept of spinning by terminology, tools and resources, tips for success, common mistakes, and a number of special rules that will help you get started in this intriguing task.

# The Results of a Spin

When first looking into spinning, you may see a bit of spintax and think it looks complicated. It is really much simpler than it looks. To begin this introduction with something a bit easier to rest your eyes on, I'm going to spin a small amount of original content and show you the results as a demonstration of the purpose of spinning.

## Original Content

By being involved in a child's education, parents dramatically increase that child's chances of graduating high school and furthering his or her education. Parents can become involved by reading to their children, talking to them about school on a regular basis, and motivating them to do well.

## Spin Result 1

A kid is much more likely to graduate high school and further his / her educational background if the mothers and fathers are involved in education from the beginning. Reading to young children, conversing with them concerning school, and inspiring them to achieve success are a couple of ways that dads and moms can be included in their children's schooling.

## Spin Result 2

When they are included in a youngster's education and learning, moms and dads drastically raise that child's chances of finishing high school and furthering his / her educational background. Moms and dads can be engaged by simply reading with their children, conversing with them about school often, and inspiring them to do well.

## Spin Result 3

By becoming engaged in a youngster's education, parents substantially raise that kid's likelihood of graduating high school and advancing his or her educational background. Reading with children, conversing with them regarding school, and inspiring them to achieve success are ways in which dads and moms can be engaged in their children's education and learning.

## Spin Result 4

A kid is far more apt to graduate high school and further their education if the parents take part in schooling from the very start. Reading with children, conversing with them regarding classes, and motivating them to be successful are some ways that parents can be included in their kid's education and learning.

---

This is from a simple first tier spin and quick word/phrase spin. With deeper spinning and more time, imagine how many ways I could express what I want to say and how many I could speak to, using varied language and the spinning concept I'm about to introduce you to.

# Choosing a Hat

In the world of content, there's a lot to be said for your fashion sense when it comes to choosing between a white hat and a black hat. At times, the line becomes a little blurry between the two and you start to wonder if grey is an option. As a professional spinner for clients, you can't always tell who's work you're spinning. It is okay to ask the client who the work belongs to, what it will be used for, and if it is being used with permission.

If someone requests that you spin content from a particular website, find out if that person is the owner or a collaborator with that site. If you get the sense that you're being asked to spin something stolen, then you need to decide if that's something you're comfortable with, sliding from your grey hat into a decidedly black one.

It is not necessary to be involved in things that you don't feel right about, just because you spin content. There are plenty of ways to use this skill to help yourself and others, typically small businesses, without harming or plagiarizing someone else.

Some feel that even spinning content that you own is an unfair technique, giving you an advantage over those who are producing genuine original content more quickly than you are able to. I have also heard it argued that there are so many spinning that a business must take it as a matter of course if their content is to be discovered and read. I personally recommend only wearing hats that you own or that have come from a reliable source.

# Common Spinning Terms

The following terms, read in the order presented, will help you to better understand the concept and terminology of content spinning before you begin.

## Spin / Spinning / Spun

To spin is to multiply unique content. You can turn a single document into any number of unique versions, which you can then compare before publishing. You do this by creating multiple options for each sentence and for each word and phrase in spintax form

## Syntax & Spintax

Syntax is a linguistics term referring to the rules and arrangement of words and phrases within sentences that are well-formed with accurate grammar. Spintax is a much newer term referring to the rules and arrangement of sentences, words, and synonyms within a spun article, with braces and vertical lines.

## Rewriting

Rewriting content is not the same as spinning content. However, to rewrite an article one time in different words is close to the equivalent of a 2nd tier spin. Rewriting skills are used in spinning as you rewrite each sentence, though you will do this sentence by sentence instead of a whole paragraph or article at a time.

## Braces and Vertical Lines

Within spintax, Braces, or "Curly Brackets" enclose the sentence and word/phrase options while Vertical Lines, or "Pipes," separate those options.

It looks like this: {Option 1|Option 2}

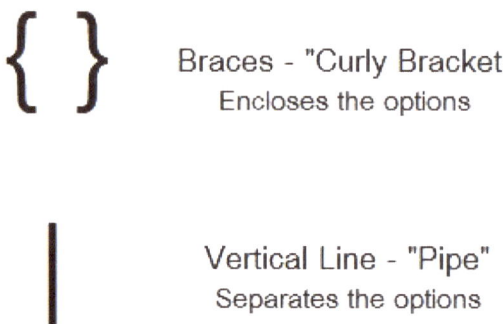

**{ }** Braces - "Curly Brackets"
Encloses the options

**|** Vertical Line - "Pipe"
Separates the options

## Tier Level

In spinning, the "tier" refers to how many options there are. If you spin to the first tier, you have not spun at all (there is only one option). If you spin to the second tier, you have rewritten the sentence or word only one time, creating two options. Following is a third tier example: {Option 1|Option 2|Option 3}

**Keep in mind:** Each additional sentence tier multiplies the work and time required to word spin.

# Word/Phrase Spinning

To word/phrase spin is to create multiple word/phrase options. In this context, "phrase" refers to two or more words which can be spun as one. Following is an example of an original sentence, word/phrase spun.

**Original Sentence:** "But mostly, I noticed that the flowers were everywhere."

**Word/Phrase Spintax:** {But|Yet|Still} {mostly|primarily}, I {noticed that|observed that} the {flowers|blossoms|blooms} were {everywhere|all over the place|almost everywhere|every place}.

**Spun Product Examples:** "Yet primarily, I observed that the blooms were all over the place."

"Still mostly, I observed that the blossoms were everywhere."

Most spinning programs recognize and underline phrases that are within the synonyms database. The program will also recommend many synonyms from within that database. If none are recommended, you can search the internet for synonyms or even check a thesaurus.

Many of the recommendations will not fit the sentence. Only choose variations that do fit in the sentence, regardless of how that sentence is spun. This is the important difference between manual and automatic spinning options. To manually spin is to consciously choose the synonyms.

# Sentence Spinning

To sentence spin is to create multiple sentence options. Sentence spinning is done to a specified tier, prior to word/phrase spinning. Following is an example of a sentence, spun to the second tier.

**Original Sentence:** "But mostly, I noticed that the flowers were everywhere."

**2nd Tier Sentence Spintax:** {But mostly, I noticed that the flowers were everywhere.|However, it is the flowers that I noticed the most. They were everywhere.}

**Spun Product Examples:** "But mostly I noticed that the flowers were everywhere."

"However, it is the flowers that I noticed the most. They were everywhere."

In this example, I spun one sentence into two sentences, which is often practical for the situation.

Only two options are available here as it has not yet been word/phrase spun. If it were spun to the 3rd tier, there would be three options prior to word/phrase spin, increasing uniqueness.

When sentence spinning, significantly rearrange the order of words and/or add new words, etc. to increase uniqueness of content. Try thinking of ways to make some sentences a bit longer or shorter than the original. Whenever you can, reverse the order of the beginning and end of the sentence and throw in something new to change it up a little bit more.

## Word/Phrase after Sentence Spin

After the sentence spin, you will word/phrase spin as described and will end up with something like the following example of a word/phrase after sentence spin.

**Example after Word/Phrase Spin:** {{But|Yet|Still} {mostly|primarily}, I {noticed that|observed that} the {flowers|blossoms|blooms} were {everywhere|all over the place|almost everywhere|just about everywhere|every place}.|{Yet|However|But|Still}, {it is the|it's the} {flowers|blooms|blossoms} {that I|I} {noticed|observed|found|acknowledged} most. {They were|These were|They're} {everywhere|all over the place|almost everywhere|just about everywhere}.}

## (blank)

Sometimes, a word or phrase can be left out of a sentence without altering the meaning. If you select the (blank) option, you will see this: {Word or Phrase|}.

Notice that there is a Vertical Bar or "Pipe" with nothing after it. This means that sometimes, that word will appear and sometimes, it will not. You can use this for sentences, too, if appropriate; but know that this does not count towards your tier level in most cases.

## Nested Spinning & Colors

Nested spinning is the term for spinning on multiple levels or tiers. Most programs will color-code your spintax based on the depth of the spin. Following is an example of deeper nested spinning with the color-coding of TBS, which we'll get to, shortly.

**2nd Tier Sentence Spintax:** {But mostly, I noticed that the flowers were everywhere.|However, it is the flowers that I noticed the most. They were everywhere.}

**Example after Word/Phrase Spin:** {{But|Yet|Still} {mostly|primarily}, I {noticed {that|}|observed that} the {flowers|blossoms|blooms} were {everywhere|all over the place|almost everywhere|just about everywhere|every place}.|{Yet|However|But|Still}, {it is the|it's the} {flowers|blooms|blossoms} {{that|which} I|I} {noticed|observed|found|acknowledged} most. {They were|These were|They're} {everywhere|all over the place|{almost|just about|} everywhere}.}

# Spinning Tools & Resources

When it comes to spinning software, you have a lot of options. Some are less expensive (some are even free) and others are more advanced and user friendly. Some require a download, though you can find online applications as well. If you are spinning for the first time, consider using one of the free options or a trial version of a paid option, if one is available.

If you are spinning as a freelancer for a client, you may be able to borrow their software to try before investing in your own. Be sure to research reviews and ratings before you invest in a spinning program.

Each spinning program will have its own instructions, both on the website and available for download. You can also look for videos related to that specific spinner online. Typically, the simple tasks are self-explanatory. You can select "New" to start a new article; you can "Open" an article you've been working on (typically saved as a Notepad document), and you can select the classic old-fashioned disk icon to save as you go.

With most spinners, you will be able to paste content into the program and go from there. With TBS and some others, you can select the Sentence or Word/Phrase option, and the program will cooperate by highlighting the right content. If it doesn't seem to be working right in TBS, selecting "Identify Synonyms" will often take care of it.

# Automatic vs. Manual Spinning

Before we discuss the various options for spinning software, we need to take a moment to discuss the options of automatic and manual spinning. There are some spinning tools and resources which only offer automatic spinning options. These will automatically choose all synonyms for each word and phrase. Manually spinning involves going through the content within the program and selecting the best synonyms.

Automatic spinning is almost never appropriate. It is typically a waste of time and money which will be quickly invested in ruining your credibility. The automatic spins always include options which do not fit within the context.

However, there is one circumstance in which automatic spinning can be useful. Some spinners choose to select the automatic spin option and to then go through the content, very carefully removing all words that do not fit with the grammar and readability of the work.

This is certainly an option, if you are seeking to have the maximum number of synonyms, though it is more time consuming, less optimized, and more prone to error. Don't be fooled by a program's promises to use "natural language detection or analysis" or "advanced artificial intelligence" to create an automatic spin; and remember that failing to remove any misplaced word can be all it takes to ruin the project.

## Uniqueness & Readability

Uniqueness and readability are the most important things when it comes to spinning content. Uniqueness refers to how unique each article is when compared to the others within the spintax and when compared with other content on the web. Many use programs to check for uniqueness, while others rely on high tiers to ensure that the uniqueness is high. Readability is the primary reason that most should avoid automatic spin options. You want your final products to be completely readable.

## The Best Spinner (TBS)

The Best Spinner, as of 2014, is widely recognized as literally the best spinning software. This is primarily because the program is user-friendly and convenient. The program makes it simple to sentence spin and word/phrase spin. It also makes it simple to generate the articles, compare them, and save them into various formats.

TBS, of course, is not a flawless program. There are glitches and risks involved and plenty of room for improvement. For example, the program suggests synonyms and will occasionally suggest words and phrases that are so far off from your intent that you'll be sincerely baffled by the suggestion.

There are also times when the program will freeze or stop working effectively when you make a mistake. A single mistake can erase all of your work! However, there are ways to minimize the risks and ensure that you make the best of The Best Spinner software. See Tips for Success and Common Mistakes.

This is not a free option, though it does have a free trial. If you are planning to spend a significant amount of time spinning content, you will find it to be worth the investment. Despite its flaws, it is generally agreed that compared to the other options available, this is the best (I am not affiliated with TBS in any way). Following are a few other options, but after discussing these, I'll be referring to The Best Spinner software throughout.

## SpinnerChief

SpinnerChief calls themselves "the real best article spinner." This specific reference to their competition further demonstrates that The Best Spinner is leading the pack as the program to beat. SpinnerChief is not a bad program, though it has fewer synonyms and is not quite as user friendly. It does have a free version and two paid version options which are less expensive than TBS and also come with free trial versions.

## Spin Rewriter

Spin Rewriter is an example of a tool which does not require a download. It is a paid service which allows you to paste or upload your article to the site, itself. It then reveals a number of synonyms for each word and phrase. This is one of the least user-friendly options, especially for the price. The program makes it fairly difficult to spin on the sentence level and to include nested spinning.

If you are spinning content for a client, you may come across someone who prefers the program or who has already invested in it, with limited experience. Thus, clients may insist that you work within their Spin Rewriter account. If you find this difficult or inconvenient, you can always use your own spinning program to begin the project and paste it into Spin Rewriter when you're finished, or prior to word/phrase spinning.

# ezArticleLink Free Article Spinner Online

With a catchy name like Free Article Spinner Online, ezArticleLink has introduced a webpage which is as advertised, free and online. This is another example of a tool which can be used without a download, though it requires no cost and is about as user friendly as Spin Rewriter. Once again, it's a program that doesn't measure up to TBS in terms of options and ease of use, but it does offer a lot for the $0 price.

It is one of the quickest options, because it doesn't require an account and if you're just looking for a quick spin, to create just one or two new articles from the original, this is a good choice. To manually spin, you simply select "Launch Assisted Spin Editor."

On that note, without an account, you can't save your work in the program. You can copy and paste the work into another document though and come back to it later by pasting it in. This site is not an option that you'll want to use if you're doing a very time consuming project; but it is a good place to experiment with spinning and to decide if it's worth investing in.

## Synonym Resources

Each example of content spinning software is equipped with a thesaurus or synonyms database to suggest synonyms for each of the words and phrases within the document. The Best Spinner is known to have the most extensive thesaurus. It updates regularly and can remember the synonyms that you've entered, if you've used them enough.

You may come across a word or phrase which does not have any suggestions. When this happens, you can think up your own or search online for synonyms. You can use your favorite online thesaurus, or you can simply enter the word and "synonyms" into a search engine.

# Challenging Phrases

Sometimes, a phrase is more challenging, like a comparison or an idiom. For example, "It was as a big as a house," "Slow and steady wins the race" or "drowning in a sea of debt." In situations like this, try to think up other options, not necessarily synonyms, but things that fit within the content and express something similar. It is also not a bad idea at all to save some of these in a document that you can refer back to - especially those that come up frequently within your industry.

**Example 1:** "It was as big as {a house|a mountain|a two story house|my house|a mansion}"

**Example 2:** "{Slow and steady wins the race.|Things will work out better if you pace yourself.|Pace yourself.|Take it slow.|Take your time.|There's no rush.}"

**Example 3:** {drowning in a sea of debt|sinking in the quicksand of debt|struggling with debt|overwhelmed by debt|buried in debt}

**Example 3 Taken Further:**
{{drowning|sinking|struggling} in {a sea|an ocean} of {debt|consumer debt}|{sinking in|struggling against|battling} the {quicksand|tides|stress} of {debt|consumer debt}|{sinking in|struggling against|battling}|{struggling with|troubled by|stressed about} {debt|consumer debt}|{overwhelmed by|consumed by|struggling with|experiencing difficulty with} {debt|consumer debt}|{buried in|sinking in|drowning in|fighting} {debt|consumer debt}}.

# TBS Color Code

Each spinning program is going to have its own color system. As I use TBS and recommend the program (though I am not affiliated), I am including the color code to help you see the various levels of spinning.

With some programs (including TBS), you can customize this system. Feel free to do so if you want. Keep in mind that it is not necessary to spin all the way to the orange or red level. You can delve into this when you feel more comfortable with deeper nested spinning.

**Black:** Not spun at all.

**Blue:** Sentence spun or word spun without prior sentence spinning. {Sentence1.|Sentence2.|Sentence3.}

**Green:** Word spun after sentence spinning. {{Words|Terms|Words and phrases} in {a sentence|sentences}.|{Sentences|A sentence} with {words|terms|words and phrases}.}

**Orange:** One level deeper; green words are turned orange with a deeper spin. {{Words|Terms|Words {and|plus|/} phrases} in {{a|your|the|one} sentence|sentences}.|{Sentences|{A|Your|The} sentence} with {words|terms|words {and|plus|/} phrases}.}

**Red:** Another level deeper; orange words are turned red with a deeper spin. {{Words|Terms|Words {and|plus|/} phrases} in {{a|your|the|{one|1|a single|individual|unique}} sentence|sentences}.|etc.}

# Tips for Success

## 1. Save A Copy!

Never spin content without saving a copy of your work elsewhere! You should frequently save the document you're working on, but you should also copy and paste it into an entirely different document as a backup, whether online or on your computer.

Anything can go wrong at any time and you can lose a lot of work. You will then have to take a break, dry your tears, and start all over. Unless you have been frequently saving a backup, in which case losing everything suddenly becomes no big deal.

## 2. Line Breaks

Create line breaks between paragraphs before you begin. This will help to make the work appear more organized and less daunting.

## 3. Question Suggested Spins

Your spinning program will suggest phrases to spin by underlining them and making it easy to select them. However, it is not always in your best interest to spin the phrases as they suggest them. Consider the following examples from TBS.

**Original:** "people <u>who suffer</u> from the flu"

**Suggestions:** "people {who suffer|who are suffering|that suffer|that are suffering} from the flu."

This time "who suffer" was underlined by TBS and these are the spins that were suggested. If, instead of highlighting the suggested "who suffer," you spin "who" and "suffer from" separately, you get much better results.

**Suggestions:** "people {who|that} {suffer from|are affected by|have} the flu."

**Example:** If "of outstanding" is underlined, you may only get: {of outstanding|of remarkable} but if you manually highlight "outstanding" by itself, you get a lot of options: "of {outstanding|exceptional|excellent|fantastic|spectacular|remarkable|superior}"

**Example:** If it says "customer happiness," you will not get much from highlighting this combination. {customer happiness|customer care}

You can either spin "customer" and "happiness" separately as mentioned above, OR you can take the one suggestion that they did give you, and spin it into a deeper nested level: "customer happiness" becomes {customer happiness|customer care}.

You then highlight "customer care" alone {customer happiness|customer care} and get many more suggestions. It will look like this when you select the suggestions for this phrase: {customer happiness|{customer care|customer service|customer support|customer satisfaction|client care}}

**Example:** "there are approximately" - To highlight the whole underlined phrase results in few options, none of them right: {there are approximately|roughly|about|around} This should be "there are {approximately|roughly|around}"

Pay attention to things like this and make sure that you are selecting the best combination of words for diverse and accurate results.

## 4. Saved Spins

If you spin multiple documents which are similar, you can save certain spins. For example, consider the following title:

"How Company Z leads Swedish and Finnish healthcare." When many articles on this topic will be spun, it is wise to save the most used spins in a separate document.

In this case, there are two good examples: {Swedish and Finnish|Finnish and Swedish|Scandinavian|Nordic|Northern European} & {healthcare|health care|medical care}

If these two spins are saved, you can copy and paste them everywhere that they belong within the article. Notice how much less work there appears to be, as all that's left to do is to word/phrase spin the blue.

{How Company Z leads {Swedish and Finnish|Finnish and Swedish|Scandinavian|Nordic|Northern European} {healthcare|health care|medical care}|How {healthcare|health care|medical care} in {Scandinavia|Scandinavian regions|Northern Europe|Sweden and Finland|Finland and Sweden|the Nordic region} is conducted by {healthcare|health care|medical care} provider, Company Z.}

# Common Mistakes

## Extra & Missing Spaces

This is something that typically occurs when you are using the tip of saving common spins and pasting them into the spaces where they belong. Watch out for them.

## Extra & Missing Line Breaks

Like extra and missing spaces, pasting into a document can cause line breaks to be removed or added. Pay attention to these things and correct them.

## Accidental Overwriting

If you select text to spin, whether it be to sentence spin or word spin, it is possible to accidentally type over the text, instead of spinning as you intended. In TBS, make sure that you see the highlighted text in the bottom box, once you've selected it. Then, make sure that your cursor is within the text entry box before typing.

If you accidentally overwrite something, you have a few options for what to do next. Selecting "Undo" will undo more work than you want it to, but this is one of the options. Another option is (if you remember the original sentence), to just put it back in. If you notice what you've done before doing anything else, you may be able to still see the original text in a box above the synonyms suggestion box at the bottom of the program screen.

## Selecting 'Undo'

Sometimes, 'Undo' is your savior. Sometimes, it is the opposite. If you've made a small mistake or accidentally overwritten text, then selecting 'Undo' can be your undoing. It may undo far more work than you intend, especially if you haven't saved recently. If this happens, select 'Redo,' and attempt to correct the small error in another way. For example, you can go back to a previously saved copy of your document and use the original text to overwrite your mistake.

## Spelling Errors

Often, spelling errors are not caused by the article spinner's deficient spelling skills. Rather, with programs like The Best Spinner, synonyms which are commonly used become synonyms that are frequently suggested. A notorious case of how this can go wrong is in the words, "health" and "heath."

A simple spell check isn't going to catch that because "heath" is a word. The best option when you discover something like this is to Ctrl F search the document for other instances of the error. Of course, a simple spell check will prevent many errors that you may miss on your way through the document.

## Capitalization Errors

Capitalization errors frequently arise due to the way the program works. It is mostly an issue with numbers and proper nouns. If you spin the numeral 11 to "eleven," "Eleven" will be capitalized, and you'll fix it manually.

If you spin the word, "America" to "USA," "US," "U.S.," etc., you'll quickly discover that you've got to go in and capitalize everything except the first letter. What you get when you simply select or type in the synonyms, in this case, is {America|Usa|Us|U.s.}. You then go back and fix it, just like the numbers. You may find that errors like this occur at other times as well, so keep your eyes open.

## Checking for Errors

One of the best ways to check for errors, aside from conducting a quick spelling check, is to select the "Spun Article" option. Depending on which spinner you use, it may have a different name, but it should be a button somewhere that you can select to view an example of what you've created. With TBS, you can hit "New Spin" repeatedly to check a number of different versions. If it reads well and everything looks right, you're good to go. If something doesn't fit, sound right, or look right, you can go back and fix it by selecting "Article" again.

## Total Destruction

Total Destruction is as good as any term to describe the horrible thing that happens when you do something, maybe paste something in or in some way mess up the spintax, and out of seemingly nowhere, the entire document disappears, except (perhaps) the bit of text that you were just working with. You can hit 'Undo' and save the day, except that you may find that you've undone far more than you wanted to.

This is a case where 'Redo' will not help you. All that will do is put you back onto the path of Total Destruction (which, if followed, means redoing the entire project). If you've been saving frequently and keeping a backup file, then this may not be so terrible.

Another instance of Total Destruction is when the program freezes. While you may be tempted to save at the earliest opportunity, this could be a fatal flaw for your project. When the program freezes, you may not know what happened, but whatever it was, it may have deleted everything. This can be fixed with an 'Undo' if the program unfreezes. However, if you happen to save while in the midst of this chaos, you might accidentally save a blank file in place of your work! If you haven't been saving frequently and haven't been keeping a backup, then you are truly screwed if any program or user error erases your work.

## Recovering from Total Destruction

The most important thing is that you recover from these Total Destruction moments. If there is no option but to start over from the beginning, or to redo a major amount of work, then take a break and come back to it when you're ready to begin again.

If spinning for a client, let the client know what has happened and request extra time to finish the project if necessary. Take it as a learning experience and a keen reminder to maintain an up-to-date backup file of your spinning work at all times.

Many are tempted to give up. You can do this. No one is going to force you to start over, and it is always an option to quit. The trouble with quitting, if you're working for a client, is that you must do so with the knowledge that you're putting someone in a real bind.

Clients would far prefer to give you extra time to finish the project over having nothing at all. Yet, forfeiting your pay and letting down a client may feel worth it, just to avoid redoing the work. This is an understandable feeling, but if you can't get past it, then spinning content is likely something that is not for you, as it does require a certain amount of resilience and dedication to satisfy a client.

# Special Rules

## The Apostrophe S Rule

Consider the following: " the company's goal"

When you highlight "**company's**" you get no suggestions. If you only highlight "**company**" you will get many suggestions.

You typically cannot highlight a word with an apostrophe without highlighting the apostrophe as well. For this reason, you can create a temporary space between the word and the apostrophe-s.

**Example:** Create a space before the 's: "company 's." Highlight "**company**" by itself, and select synonyms: {company|organization|business|agency} 's.

Then, remove the space before the 's: {company|organization|business|agency}'s.

Remember to delete any words that don't work with the 's: {company|organization|agency}'s

# Hyphen Rules

Hyphenated words may not have any or many suggestions, but you can come up with your own, spin each half of the hyphenated word separately, or spin the hyphenated word into two non-hyphenated words and spin them separately then.

**Examples for adjective:** "mouse-like"

Option 1. Spin with alternate options: {mouse-like|mousy|like a mouse|quiet|sneaky}

I included 'quiet' and 'sneaky' as alternates here, because - depending on the context - either could be an alternate adjective for the subject.

Option 2. Spin each half of the hyphenated word separately: {mouse|rodent|rat|rabbit}-{like|resembling|looking}

Note, that I included 'rat' and even 'rabbit' as a reminder that the words do not always have to mean the same thing, especially when using comparisons / similes / metaphors. If it fits with the context and intent, then use it.

Option 3. Spin hyphenated words into an option without a hyphen .{mouse-like|mouse like} Then, spin the two options individually: {{mouse|rodent|rat|rabbit}-{like|resembling|looking}|{mouse|rodent|rat||rabbit} {like|resembling|looking}}

Option 4: If applicable to the context, you can also spin the hyphen itself like this: {-|/|}

## A & An Rules

It would make sense for the 'a' or 'an' to be connected with the word that follows it in suggested spins, because it is the word that follows which determines which of these options you need. However, the programs will often do it the other way around and underline 'a' or 'an' as the last word of a phrase.

**Example:** "They are an established company."

When you spin 'established,' you need the 'a' or 'an' to be accurate. So, do not take their underlining suggestion to spin "They are an" together.

Instead, spin: "They are" and then spin "an established."

In this way, you end up with "{an established|a well-established|a popular} company"

Sometimes, you will get fewer suggestions when you select the 'a' or 'an' along with the following word. To address this issue, you can do the following:

Spin with one 'an' word and one 'a' word: "{an established|a popular}" Then, spin 'established' alone, with only other vowel-beginning words. Then, spin 'popular' alone, with only other consonant-beginning words.

**Result:** "{an {established|accomplished}|a {popular|well-established|successful}} company."

## List Spinning Rules

Spin lists by rearranging their order, before you spin the actual words within the list

**Example:** "They bought Cheerios, apples, cookies, soup, and peanut butter."

"They bought {apples, peanut butter, soup, cookies, and Cheerios|cookies, Cheerios, soup, peanut butter, and apples|soup, peanut butter, Cheerios, cookies, and soup.}

You do not need to spin every possible version (unless it's only a list of three). Just mix them up a bit. You can then spin the items within the list.

"They bought {{apples|fruit|cherries|strawberries|peaches}, {peanut butter|PB|Jiff|jelly|peanut butter and jelly}, {soup|ramen|chicken noodle soup|Campbells tomato soup}, {cookies|Oreos|chocolate chip cookies|candy}, and {Cheerios|cereal|Rice Krispies|Apple Jacks|Fruit Loops|Frosted Flakes}|cookies, Cheerios, soup, peanut butter, and apples|soup, peanut butter, Cheerios, cookies, and soup.}"

Use Copy/Paste where practical.

# Spinning with a Purpose

When it comes to spinning content, there are a number of different ways to use the skill, including ways that are near to your own heart. Consider the things that you're interested in, the things that you support, and the things you'd like to learn about.

There are people in all fields, in all industries, and in all places looking for excellent spun content of a particular variety that you might be able to provide, and you might even have fun with it!

If you've got your own site, your own cause, and your own content to distribute and want to do so on your own, then this could be just the tool and skill that you need to avoid spending thousands more on the amount of content that you need to produce.

When it comes to making money, there are many opportunities for anyone who is willing to invest the time and effort into a high quality spin. Everywhere you go, you'll find someone in need of high quality unique content with a budget and schedule to meet.

While the skill of content spinning is not so difficult to learn and it is certainly one of the simpler ways to make money online, a truly reliable spinner is hard to come by. You can make a name for yourself in the freelancing world just by being responsive, responsible, and willing to learn! I hope that this book helps you in whichever direction you choose to take the information.

# About the Author

Johnna Russell is an author, editor, and web content specialist. She was born in 1985 and raised in Michigan and Texas. Currently residing in Michigan with her family, Johnna is a very busy wife, learning coach, and mother of three. She fell into her niche purely by accident while wandering aimlessly along roads less traveled by.

www.ingramcontent.com/pod-product-compliance
Lightning Source LLC
Chambersburg PA
CBHW040813200526
45159CB00022B/754